Your Survival Guide

Your Home in DIVORCE

Michael Williamsen

Names, characters, places and stories have been based on true stories, but, names and incidents have been altered to protect the innocent and of course the writer!

Copyright © 2019 Michael Williamsen Productions

ISBN: 978-0-9985376-3-4

DEDICATION

This book is dedicated to past, current, and future friends, colleagues, clients, and family who shared their darkest moments, fears, desires and experiences to give hope and solutions to help others going through the many issues of divorce and real estate.

Why This Book Was Written

Many clients, friends, and families charged into divorce blindly, only to suffer greatly emotionally, health-wise, and financially. Self-respect was replaced with feelings of failure and guilt. These mistakes gave them reasons not to forgive themselves. By the time they figured out what to do, an excessive amount of the money was gone. It was time. I felt compelled to write this book.

This book will empower you with knowledge and understanding from many who have experienced divorce and real estate issues. You will learn many aspects of a real estate transaction which will help you to reduce risk, stress, anxiety, and avoid future regrets.

Become your own best advocate. Learn how to find the facts. Ask smart questions to the pros.

Find answers about real estate most people don't even know to ask the questions. Make informed decisions. Avoid many of the pitfalls.

Avoid becoming just another survivor or a victim.

Find answers concerning real estate issues that most don't even know enough to ask about.

Find comfort knowing you have a plan.

WARNING this book is not giving legal, financial or any other advice. Codes, regulations, case history, tax laws, and many issues vary from state to state, county to county, judge to judge, frequently changing, creating clouds of expensive confusion.

This book is not providing any advice on custody of children, financial, psychological, or anything other than real estate. Though, finding peace of mind and clarity on your real estate may help other aspects of your life.

Please consult with appropriate professionals before taking action.

This is not a "how to" or "do-it-yourself" book, but hopefully to make you aware of situations and possibilities, seek out proper help, and act in an efficient and informed process.

Special Thanks To

Steve Gainer - Real Estate Attorney, Contributor on dealing with attorneys.

Alice Robertson – Home Organization Specialist

Joan Carlson – Cover Design

Jami Williamsen – Cover Design

Bonnie Coren – Relationship Advisor, Masters in Psychology, Contributor, Editor

Lori Salinas – MA, MFT, professional witness in family court, Contributor

Kelley Way – Estate Attorney, Contributor

Charylu Roberts – Editor and Publisher

Linda Zanides – Zanides Public Relations

Marcia Mills – Editor, Real Estate Agent

Jim Sagorac – Real Estate Agent, Contributor, Contractor and Author of *"Building Your Dream House with Sticks & Stones, & Color Tones."*

Vladlena McClure – Real Estate Agent, Developer Investor

Fernando Gomez – Contributor and Editor

Laura – My late wife, for all the memories

A few people like you:

"The fear of the unknown and potentially losing my home in my divorce was extremely stressful. I highly recommend this book, it guided me in becoming my own advocate and pursue with courage, what I wanted. This informative read is a must if you are in the throws of divorce."
Dee Sangster, Child Care Provider and Divorcee

Whether you own a mansion or rent a small apartment, breaking up the family home is a traumatic experience to be taken seriously. This book is extremely valuable, a must read. It will assist you in making informed decisions about your home during a divorce.
Bonnie Coren, Relationship Advisor

"My divorce was horrible. The worst part of it was dealing with my own attorney. The best part was Michael's patience, understanding of the situation. I felt he was truly on my side."
Roberta, Artist, Divorcee, Marin County

"Michael's advice is always direct and to the point, never self-serving."
Len Nibbi, San Rafael Developer

"Michael Williamsen's book is well written, insightful and concise. It offers a solid blueprint of practical and preventative financial advice and plenty of real estate gems of wisdom to protect and safeguard your biggest asset, your home! Highly recommend and a must read for any homeowner!"
James Sagorac, Real Estate Agent, Divorcee, Developer, and Writer of "Building Your Dream House with Sticks & Stones, & Color Tones."

"Be mindful of changes in mood and behavior; be aware of your reactions that may make situations worse. These negative mindsets can affect how one makes decisions."
Lori A Salinas, MA, MFT, professional witness and consultant in family courts

"Paying property taxes IS an obligation…
Overpaying is NOT." *Joy Hurtig, Vice President,
Property Tax Reduction Strategies*

"Everyone should have a copy of Michael
Williamsen's new book! He touches on all aspects
of our lives offering invaluable insider Tips on
How To Save Ourselves from losing money. We
are Very lucky Michael wrote this book. He
shares his experience intelligently, to the point
and with humor! Order your book fast at
Amazon! You will thank him and so will your
pocketbook!"
*Linda Zanides, owner Zanides Public Relations
and Divorcee*

"A wide range of real estate experience and
education give Mike an endless supply of
strategies and solutions. He is consistently
turning his clients' problems into opportunities
and his clients get the rewards. A pro's pro!"
*David Kessner – Real Estate Broker/Investor, and
Divorcee*

TABLE OF CONTENTS

INTRODUCTION

CHAPTER 1   Follow Your Heart?
Truth or Dare?

CHAPTER 2   Who is Really On Your Side?
Do they have their own agendas?

CHAPTER 3   What Is Your Plan?
You do have a plan, don't you?

CHAPTER 4   Who Owns Your House?
The many types of ownership

CHAPTER 5   What Your Property Worth?
Who do you believe?

CHAPTER 6   What Is Your Property
**   REALLY Worth?**
   Debts, liabilities, repairs, and unsightly
   issues

CHAPTER 7   Evaluation
   This is not a test. This is your life

CHAPTER 8   Keep Your House?
   To keep or not to keep. That Is the
question

CHAPTER 9   Sell?
   Is this an end or a beginning?

CHAPTER 10   Where Are You Going?
   Your New Home and How to Get There

A Personal Message from the Author

About the Author

Michael Williamsen

INTRODUCTION

What is there to be afraid of?

"We have nothing to fear but fear itself."

Franklin D. Roosevelt.

Fear and greed are the two biggest human motivators. Divorce combines the two. With the proper knowledge, fear can be turned into the understanding that fear is a subconscious alert to our bodies, minds, and souls, that something very important is happening.

> **Insider Tip**: Make a list of all your fears. Elaborate. Clarity is a great start to solutions.

Have you ever stayed awake all night worrying about something, to find out in the morning your concern had already worked itself out?

15

Divorce could be the worst form of self-destruction we bring upon ourselves. Doubt, betrayal, guilt, confusion, fear, risk, drama, loss, anxiety, and almost every type of emotional baggage we can imagine, and can confuse our every move.

Emotions raise expectations causing anger, revenge, and bitterness. Due to the loss, we have hopes for compensation for taking:

"the best years of my life."

Children and pets get caught in an emotional tug-of-war confused why they are losing their home and family existence. Why is it kids always have to pay for the mistakes of their parents?

Many people have stated divorce was the worst experience of their lives. Cold and callous as this sounds, looking at the big picture, you might wonder if the worst parts of their divorce were caused by themselves. Their expectations, emotional roller coasters, changes of heart, fear, guilt, self-doubt, and anxiety of an unknown future... it just doesn't stop. And, it clouds the tasks at hand.

Caught in the crossfire of conflicted family and friends, professional advisors waging a war of unknown outcome and cost, it is no wonder people are confused and angry.

This book is not about your personal anger, fears, resentment or any emotional concerns, though, they are certainly valid. This book will help you <u>cope</u> with issues, but that is not the main topic. Selling your house is not one of the five stages of recovery. Keep them separate.

Five Stages of Anger
Denial
Anger
Bargaining
Depression
Acceptance

If blood is thicker than water, then money is thicker than blood. And, anger and hatred are thicker than money.
Michael Williamsen

Don't discount your emotions, but also don't let them guide your decisions. You have family, friends, therapists, counselors, and bartenders to share your feelings.

Read the above paragraphs, again and again, until you get that. This book will help relieve a lot of the confusion, self-doubt about pending decisions, anxiety about questions un-answered and questions you may not even know to ask.

This book is about your money, security, and future. This book is about making wise decisions, based on truth and facts. Let your guilt guide you into making practical choices. Crave knowledge. Many friends, family, and professionals will have advice, some may have their own agendas in that advice. Most will not know your full circumstances. You may not know your full situation yet either.

"Courage is not overcoming fear, but,

moving forward in spite of fear."

Become your own best advocate. Do it yourself. "Self" is the crucial word in self-esteem, self-confidence, self-discipline, and self-respect. The fear and anxiety caused by divorce have most likely dented if not shattered these life skills. Here is your first chance to re-build them.

Start your new life with the confidence and peace of mind in having made the best decisions possible.

Michael Williamsen

CHAPTER ONE

Follow your heart?

This concept is an epic line for advice given in love songs and poetry. This is not the not the theme you want for this chapter in your story unless your mission is to create a best-selling autobiography of expectations are met with disappointment and self-destruction.

This concept is not new. A Biblical prophet wrote over 2000 years ago:

> "The heart is deceitful above all
> things, and desperately wicked:
> who can know it?" *Jerimiah 17:9*

Make informed decisions with your brain, with information, strategies, facts, and truths. Plan out the business of your future as a business.

"Information is Power."

"If you think education is expensive, try ignorance."

A well-known scene from the movie <u>A Few Good Men</u>:

> JESSUP (Jack Nicholson): You want answers?
> KAFFEE (Tom Cruise): I think I'm entitled to them.
> JESSUP: You want answers?
> KAFFEE: I want the truth!
> JESSUP: YOU CAN'T HANDLE THE TRUTH.

A common quote about the truth:
"What you don't know won't hurt you."

Seriously? The truth is harsh, bold, often unspeakable, and sometimes almost impossible to accept. Denying it can be costly and may destroy you; you just won't know any better. One of

Jesus's apostle John wrote a common misunderstood statement:

"The truth shall set you free." John 8:32

The truth may or may not set you free, but deceiving yourself will certainly free you of your well-being and assets. The truth is also the source of peace in knowing the good, the bad, and the evil. The real killer is worrying about things you don't even know enough to worry over.

"It's easier to pass judgment when not confused by the facts."
Michael Williamsen

It seems we want to cling onto the first statement we see or hear that we want to be the truth. This is what advertising is all about. Just read the label on your "healthy boxed cereal." Facebook is filled with those investing their time supporting a headline without an understanding, or even wanting an understanding of the issue.

No longer think of your house as your home. It is a house, a box on a piece of dirt, likely an expensive combination. Most often it is the most substantial investment of your

> **Insider Tip**: Real estate agents often call a seller's home a **house** to take off the emotional attachment. They describe the house as <u>a</u> **home** to buyers to create the emotional attachment.

life and probably the most significant source of money for your new future. Sometimes it's easier to imagine dealing with this property as you would for a friend or family member. Don't you deserve the same honesty with yourself?

Keeping or selling your house is not about winning. It's not about justice. It's not about getting more than your share, it's about <u>not losing</u> your share.

This is just about taking care of yourself, posturing yourself with the best financial position for your future. Don't be resentful that your future ex-spouse may get some of the proceeds. Your concern is your proceeds for your future.

If you can't give up on your anger, save it for later disputes. Anger causes confusion and poor decisions, creating or allowing costly mistakes. You can fight for justice later in the settlement hearing, plus you will have more money for more ammunition. People will dig in on the last line of defense.

"It's not just about the money."

<u>YES IT IS!</u> At the end of fight, all the sleepless nights and tears will leave you empty. What you are really fighting over is the house, money, and the stuff. And with this, you will begin your future. All the anger will not be resolved. Think of everything else in your real estate transaction as a distraction.

"Its about the principles (morals)"

It is about the principle, but, "principle" as in equity in your house.

There is a famous attorney limerick:

"Sure, you can get justice, how much justice can you afford?"

Displaying emotion shows weakness in the business environment. This is the business of your future.

A privately held luxury real estate firm was owned by husband Ted and wife Alice. Real estate is tough on relationships. Ted and Alice were no exception. They hired a divorce attorney who wrote up a settlement agreement separating their assets, which included the business. They signed, settled, and continued on with their very successful individual lives and careers.

Daniel owned a high-profile real estate firm. His wife Carol used her marketing and sales skills to bring the company to great success while Daniel pursued other interests. They separated. Carol hired Ted's attorney who handed her Ted and Alice's settlement agreement as an immediate answer to their pending crisis.

Daniel, making it known that he is the rightful owner of the company, made scathing accusations against Carol on social media causing several top agents to leave to avoid the drama and potential damage to their reputations and the company's value.

The court decreed Carol to continue to manage the company. Daniel received a gag order as his blabbering in public was greatly damaging the company's productivity and value. Daniel continued his war on social media.

In the end, the court awarded sole ownership of the company to Daniel who immediately fired Carol. Agents loyal to Carol, many who had never even met Daniel, fled the company. The damage to the company was catastrophic. The company is allegedly under bankruptcy. Keep in mind, these two were highly successful real estate brokers.

Tips from Chinese military general Sun Tzu in his book "The Art of War:"

> He will win who knows when to fight and when not to fight.

> There is no instance of a country having benefited from prolonged warfare.

> The greatest victory is that which requires no battle.

Insider Tip: Lori Salinas, MA/MFT is a Mental Health professional. She is also a professional witness and consultant in family and mental health courts. Lori offers the following advice:

Often, while going through a contested or un-contested divorce, there are other issues that can arise or negative behaviors that become more apparent, besides the financial end of things.

A Divorce can be a traumatic experience. There are many changes that a person goes through from the changing of the family dynamic to feelings of loss and emptiness.

While the financial issues are always a concern, the heart and mind need tending to as well. Be mindful of changes in mood and behavior; be aware of your reactions that may make situations worse. These negative mindsets can affect how one makes decisions, therefore, it is suggested that people find support such as therapy or divorce support groups to release tension and find closure in moving on from the old and looking forward to the new way of life.

The splitting of the family dynamic is considered a life-changing event, which should be taken just as seriously. Go to PsychologyToday.com and look for articles and support groups or therapists in your area.

Lori A Salinas, MA/MFT

Jane has been separated from the son of a wealthy family for two years. She lives in a house the family owns and is letting her stay in while the divorce goes on. The husband/son is staying in the house that he and Jane own together. Jane describes her divorce action as "waiting it out," as apparently, "nothing is going on with the divorce proceedings."

Wait until you get through the next chapter to decide if you agree that Jane is OK just waiting it out.

Watch the movie, *War of the Roses,* and decide which side betrays the ending you prefer. Hopefully, neither.

Information is Power.
Ignorance is a DISASTER.

CHAPTER TWO

Who is Really on Your Side?

Do they have their own agendas?

Insider Tip: Bonnie Coren is a Relationship Advisor with a Masters Degree in Psychology. Bonnie offers the following tips:

If blood is thicker than water (meaning that family bonds are stronger than bonds with friends), than surely money is thicker than blood. Anyone who has gone through divorce or Estate battles will agree in somber approval.

That said, usually both family and good friends have your best interests at heart. Unfortunately, they also bring their own agendas, either consciously or unconsciously. They will share with you their valuable experiences, their hopes for you, and what they truly believe to be the Truth. It would be wise for you to consider their advice. Be sure to take into account, they are not professionals. They are biased and clearly not objective. Cherish their wisdom, but also realize they do not see the whole picture. They do not know your complete situation or the best way to attain your goals.

Professionals also have their own agendas and slants on situations. They get paid well for sharing their knowledge, this advice is charged hourly. Be careful in this regard, often litigation is simply settled because it has become too costly to continue.

When choosing a professional keep in mind what you are looking for, the best ones are calm, objective, and good communicators. They should be good team players, who work well with other professionals who are also representing you. They will explain your options in a practical and non-judgmental process.

You can do your part in getting the most out of your professionals by being cooperative and by being part of the solution, not part of the problem. Be sure to give your professionals complete information so they can evaluate your situation to the best of their abilities.

Bonnie Coren, MA

Laura and George quickly came to a decision: she got the house, he got the business. The couple's attorneys battle ferociously over what was left. Laura started dating her attorney attempting to entice him to better represent her. The couple's cash disappeared and they realized they really didn't have much more than the house and business.

> **Insider Tip:** A good idea is to go into every meeting with a written agenda. Take notes so that you don't have to pay for a call about something you already discussed. When the list is completed, leave and note the time you were there.

Laura had to take out an equity line to bring her attorney fees current. Her attorney retired, moved away, and the case settled – so Laura thought.

She fell in love with a new man who unraveled that Laura's divorce was neither settled, nor recorded as final--he unwittingly had been dating a married woman. After finalizing Laura's divorce, they got married a few years later.

Game of Thrones character Lord Baylish, (Littlefinger) in his course of courting the much younger, acting Queen of the North, Sansa Stark, used his wisdom in attempts to win her favor:

"Sometimes when I try to understand a person's motives, I play a little game. I assume the worst; what's the worst reason they could possibly have for saying what they say and doing what they do.

Then I ask myself: well, does that reason explain with they say and what they do?"

Unfortunately for Lord Baylish, Sansa used this advice to uncover <u>his</u> own motives. This may be the way you want to evaluate your team.

YOUR TEAM

Family and friends. They are great for emotional support. They may share with you advice on issues and maybe their personal experiences. Remember, they most likely do not have all the facts that you do. They may or may not give the best advice, but they are great to bounce issues off of, at least bring things to mind, and certainly less costly than the professionals. Friends and family may speak things from their hearts with best intentions which you may find offensive. Please forgive them as they will be an important part of your new life.

Tax Professionals. Seek professional help on tax issues. Prepare with as much financial information as you can, including documents on your house such as purchase price (original HUD final closing document can be obtained from the escrow company), cost of improvements, an

> **Insider Tip**: There are legal advice companies who, for a monthly fee, provide almost unlimited legal advice. They are great to bolster your knowledge of your legal situation and limit time with your attorney in the future.

estimate of current property value, and tax statements. Write out a list of questions. Write down the answers.

Real Estate Agent. Don't let them sell you into making the most common mistakes picking an agent:

1) **Using the agent who gives you the highest price**. The two ends of the spectrum are the agent who tries to "buy the listing" by offering an

inflated price with hidden plans on reducing the list price later, and the low-ball estimate to get a quick commission, possibly by enticing multiple offers. Not every property is suitable for multiple buyers and won't attract multiple offers. Ultimately, it is the buyers who determine what the house sells for. The list price is to entice potential buyers to look at the property. An intelligent list price will bring the best buyer in the shortest amount of time.

2) **Not using a local agent.** There is a lot of insider knowledge that local agents gain just through personal experience and being around other agents. The lack of this specialized knowledge can cost you money and add miscommunication and confusion, and ultimately, the loss of a timely, professional, choreographed sale. One buyer's agent did not know it was customary for seller to pay the transfer tax in San Francisco. He checked the box in the contract that buyer will pay all transfer

taxes. The buyer unsuspectingly payed over $22,000 in transfer taxes.

An agent based in Marin County with a San Francisco listing may post the listing directly onto the San Francisco MLS. However, Zillow will not post the listing unless it is posted on the Marin County MLS BAREIS. Insiders know this as well as many other situations costing sellers money.

3) **Using a friend.** Unless this friend is a seasoned agent whom you trust completely, this is not the time to be kind to a friend. This is the time your friend needs to be supportive of you including using an agent who is the most qualified to help you in your own best interests.

4) **Using the Big Gun**. Selecting an agent because they are the biggest producer, great salespeople, has a fancy suit, nice car or flashy appearances may backfire. Their

sales skills will be used on you getting you to sign the listing agreement, offers, and other documents. Most real estate training is about sales and marketing and leveraging processes to increase their productivity, not customer service.

Estate Attorney. Selling or keeping the house may affect your Trust or cause you to get one. Trusts provide a lot of benefits. More on that later.

Divorce Attorney. Some couples start out on a do-it-yourself path. It's usually money and/or kids that bring the hired guns into action. Do you remember the scene where Indiana Jones has an opponent pull out his sword? Indiana Jones pulls out his pistol and shoots the opponent. You are in a shooting match. Get a gunslinger. Remember, they may have the gun pointed at you too.

Many attorneys are nice and capable people. They are friendly, glad to listen to your issues, sympathize, and show kindness. You are paying for this kindness by the hour—you are not paying them for emotional support.

In sending out rough drafts of this book, there were many responses to the likes of:

"My divorce was the worst thing ever in my life. My own attorney was the worst part of my divorce."

Lida, charmed by her divorce attorney Richard, began dating him, thinking he would take special care of her.

Insider Tip: For a small monthly fee, Legal Shield provides free legal advice over about 80 fields of law. This is a great place to get informed and test your questions. www.legalshield.com

She got the house, kids, and a huge bill from the law firm. She had to take out a hard-money 2nd mortgage to pay her attorney fees.

Insider Tip: Steve Gainer is a business and real estate attorney, located in Marin County practicing throughout the San Francisco Bay Area. While he doesn't handle divorce cases, he had some very helpful advice on hiring and working with divorce attorneys, as well as, attorneys providing other legal services. When asked to review this chapter sent back this reply:

Shop around for attorneys. Most will give a free consultation. So, ask for this. And ask other questions of concern to you, such as an attorney's willingness to try to reach compromises without "going nuclear" with a full trial. You want to ask the same questions to see if the answers are consistent among the attorneys you interview.

You don't want to get into a legal dispute over attorney's fees that exceed way over what you expected. It will be like being a rooster going into the wolves' den demanding them to stop eating your hens.

If you think your attorney is a nice guy and will be fair to you, still ask him or her for references from prior clients.

Many attorneys "put on a show" with beautiful offices. But this doesn't indicate an attorney's effectiveness. A "pound of image" does not equal even "one ounce of effective performance". And remember who is being billed for the money to support this prestigious office: YOU.

Understand that while there are greedy attorneys who want to "milk" clients for fees as much as possible, in most lawsuits, attorneys including divorce attorneys, have another motivation which is more "innocent" but can lead to the same problem for clients: these attorneys have big egos and want to impress everyone with how smart and tough they are. So, they put in large amounts of billable time and spend large amounts of client money as "costs" on "expert advisors" and "expert witnesses" so the attorney can satisfy their big egos or "business advertising" needs. BUT THE CLIENT IS PAYING FOR THE ATTORNEY'S "EGO TRIP" and advertising.

So, "head off" this "lawyer ego problem", etc. by making clear to the attorney that you have some clear practical goals to reach (achievable in the general American system of justice–see Point (2) below) and will be satisfied reaching these goals as closely as possible, EVEN IF this means "making nice" with the other attorney or the "adversary" on the other side, and even making some compromises you can live with. And further make clear that you will appreciate the abilities of your attorney if these clear practical goals are reached, and your friends will be equally impressed later.

For YOUR OWN part in taking the steps just mentioned, YOU must examine the situation you are in, your true feelings about your situation, and focus on what you need. Don't become disillusioned by dreamy expectations or paranoid over some exotic nighttime fantasies. Become realistic sooner than later.

A judge or jury or an arbitrator (a privately hired "judge") is permitted to consider, generally limited to: awarding you money; other property you are entitled to be paid for something you contributed to or are otherwise entitled to; other property you lost or were denied; (in the case of divorce) financial support and optimum living situation for a non-working spouse and for younger children of a divorcing couple.

Keep in mind that in some realm beyond our earthly existence you may get the satisfaction of revenge, infliction of exquisite sadistic torture, etc. on whomever "did you wrong" and with whom you are now locked in a dispute with, but (again) the closest you may get to this goal here is by running up fees for both you and your adversary, or creating life-scarring fees on children.

When you go into your attorney's office bring absolutely everything you think pertains to your case. Even the stuff against your case--it will come out sooner than later. Don't let your attorney get caught in your lie. In that situation your attorney <u>will</u> need to spend a lot of billable time trying to deal with your (exposed) lie and your attorney will be less positive about you since you have now put the attorney in an embarrassing situation with the other attorney or, even worse, a judge. Sooner is a lot cheaper when it comes to most key disclosures that are likely to be "found out" eventually.

Other questions you should consider asking potential attorneys:

(1)   Retainer – does the agreement allow the attorney to go over the retainer without written approval from the client?

(2)   If you are getting legal services from a firm of lawyers:

(i)   Ask what the hourly rate is for each lawyer working on your case, and for each paralegal.

(ii)   Ask how you will be charged for "conferences" or "meetings" among lawyers-paralegals in the firm when all are together to discuss your case.

Attorneys practicing in California cannot charge fees which are "unconscionable", but this vague standard leaves a lot of room for some very high fees.

(3)   Take notes.

(4)   Write down dates, times, and who was there.

If you ask a question and the attorney says, "I don't know, we will look into it", ask if this involves basic information which an attorney in the area you are involved in ought to know. If so, why the attorney should be charging you for basic education in this area. You don't want to pay for education the attorney should have had before you walked into the attorney's office. BUT on the other hand, don't expect an attorney to know every issue in your situation. Legal rules in most areas are very large in number, often not immediately clear, or constantly change.

Also, be wary of a "know it all" lawyer. This can be a warning sign of phoniness or carelessness about the complexity of legal rules.

Steve Gainer, Real Estate Attorney

A Good Bartender. Often a necessity on your team.

CHAPTER THREE

What Is Your Plan?

An hour of planning can save many hours of future work, frustration, and mistakes. Treat your house like a business – profit, loss, time invested, and future return. Start with the known facts, assets and liabilities to come up with a focused, written plan based on objective information.

> **Insider Tip**: A plan is written on paper. Anything else is a dream or wish.

A single man bought a one-bedroom, bachelor-pad condo. He remodeled the condo, doing a great deal of the work himself. His talents were recognized by a young woman. They married and bought a new house together to raise their family using a $150k equity line on the condo as the down-payment on their new home.

He kept the condo as a rental. Rentals provide great tax breaks. Their expenses were written off, plus, the structure was depreciated ten of the allowed 27.5 years.

He sold the condo barely covering the first mortgage and the equity line. He had lost all the receipts for the remodeling and couldn't deduct the expenses. His own labor did not count towards the cost of improvements. The ten years of depreciation had to be recaptured and added back into the taxable gain.

Not only was there no equity in the property, but he also had to pay taxes on the $200k gain which calculated to about $85k.

All of this could have been avoided with a knowledge of the tax codes and consequences and a plan.

Your plan could be as simple as:

1) What do you want?
    a. What will it cost you to get it?
    b. Who can help you?
    c. What are your options?
    d. What will happen if you don't get it?
2) What are you willing to sacrifice?
    a. Prioritize what you want.
3) What are the facts?
4) How can you apply the facts to get what you want?

What Are the Facts?

"Just the facts, ma'am."
Dragnet Sgt. Joe Friday

Bigger expectations result in bigger disappointments. The fact is, Sgt. Friday, according to Wikipedia, never said this quote. But then why cloud the issue with too many facts.

What About a Credit Plan?

One large asset that gets dismissed all too fast is credit. Spouses leaving divorces with destroyed credit is almost a right-of-passage. You must protect your credit. If you think not, you will very possibly get the chance to wish you had. Find a good credit counselor. Speak to a loan broker as soon as possible.

Cancel joint accounts.

Transfer billing addresses to your new address. Late payments don't care if you got the bill or not.

Open your own credit cards in only your name.

File a Fraud Alert on your credit. Alerting one credit agency will alert the other two. You don't want your ex-spouse opening up credit in your name. If you fear desperately to protect your credit ask for a Credit Freeze.

If one spouse is planning to buy out the other, open a credit line or get the new mortgage as soon as possible. You don't want all your plans messed up by a couple of missed bills forcing you to sell.

Alimony and child support affect both spouses' ability to get a loan.

CHAPTER FOUR

Who Really Owns Your House?

The many types of ownership

If you know absolutely how your property's title is held, you can skip to the VALUE CHAPTER. As of this writing, a lot of the public records online do not report all the details of real property ownership.

> **Insider Tip:** A real estate agent can get their favorite escrow officer to look up your property ownership and liens as a service.

Cathy's first husband played stay-at home dad while she pursued her rock-star career. A tour cancelled early, and she planned to surprise her husband. She opened the master bath door to hear a woman's voice call out from behind the shower curtain, "honey, you're home early." Cathy didn't hand the mistress a towel. She did lose the house, custody of her child, and paid alimony and child support for many years.

True love found Cathy at the altar the second time. He traveled and loved the life of the rich and famous, especially the groupies. She felt inadequate and tried harder to win sole custody of his affection. His attempt to rape her daughter ended her matrimonial bliss and started an addiction to drugs.

Cathy's third husband traveled on the road, managed her career, and tended to the safety of various personal business. On one homecoming, he casually mentioned he had filed for divorce. "Ok, then get out of my house," she ranted. "Sorry honey," he responded. "The house is in a corporation, which is my name, as well as the other properties and all the investments." Your car and the lease for the rehearsal studio are still in your name. By the way the rent payment is due this coming Thursday." Cathy is currently living in the music studio while she tries to find a way to regain ownership of her music and rights to play concerts.

Sole Ownership

Sole ownership, also known as ownership in severalty, is the most common way to hold property as a single person. Once married, this property can stay as Sole Ownership, but several things can challenge this ownership. If the owner uses community property funds to pay for property expenses (called commingling), there may be a cloud on the title and ownership, possibly or partially, turning the property into community property.

In selling a property as Sole Ownership, spouses are most often required to sign a Quitclaim Deed acknowledging no claim to the property.

Sole Ownership has no secret advantages or special tax breaks. If the owner dies, the property goes to probate. It will be distributed by will instructions if a will exists. Without a will, the property would be distributed by court instructions, usually a simple formula to distribute amongst survivors, including children and spouses.

Insider tip: Wills are flimsy and easy to create. The epic story of an elderly person on their death-bed willing everything to the new love of their life is not a joke. It happens all the time and is very hard to contest. Challengers must prove the will was signed at a moment of lack of mental capacity. Even in times of overwhelming medical or mental trauma, the phrase "random act of cognizance" is almost impossible to disprove.

One Marin heiress's father, worth over $50,000.000 died. His young bride of two years showed up with a will granting all the father's property to the bride. The daughter and disgruntled heiress fought. After a million dollars in attorney fees and uncountable bills for treatment of depression and anxiety, the heiress withdrew her claim.

Community Property

In California, Nevada, Louisiana, Wisconsin, Texas, Arizona, Washington, Idaho and New Mexico, spouses, without other direction, take the title as Community Property. Each spouse owns title to half the property. In the event of a death, a spouse's ownership can be passed to anyone by a will.

Insider Tip: Personal debts may also be included in community property. If you run up a visa card on power tools or gifts to disadvantaged children, your personal debt may be Community Property and your spouse may be held responsible for 50%, and the other way around as well. Know what you are getting into.

A particular advantage is that community property assets willed to a surviving spouse receive a new stepped-up basis at market value on the date of death. In 1987, the IRS extended this community property stepped-up basis advantage to husbands and wives holding joint tenancy titles in community property states.

A step-up in basis reflects the changed value of an inherited asset. For example, Bob bought a house for $100,000. His cost basis was $100,000. Years later, the value of his property was $500,000. Had Bob sold, he would have a taxable gain of $400,000. Bob died. His son Bryan inherited the property and Bryan's new cost basis was stepped up to $500,000. Bryan sold the property for $500,000. Bryan did not pay any taxes on the sale as the property value was "stepped up" to $500,000. Had Bryan sold the property for $600,000, he would have had a taxable gain of $100,000.

To qualify, IRS Revenue Ruling 87-98 requires spouses to acknowledge in writing to each other that their joint tenancy property is also community property.

Tenants in Common

Tenants in Common is most common for unmarried partners who have chosen to co-own property. They may divide the interest any way they want, not precisely equal, and the shares are specified on the deed. This is common with investors, and it may be several investors. They may sell, transfer the deed, or grant by will their shares to whomever they want. This may also be a downside as the old partners may get stuck with a new undesirable partner. Tenants in Common is also subject to probate and may expose the shareholders to a partition lawsuit where one partner forces all the partners to sell.

A deed, title, or other legally binding property ownership document spells out the terms of either tenancy in common or joint tenancy.

Joint Tenancy

This type of holding title is most common between husbands and wives and among family members in general since it allows the property to pass to the survivors without going through probate (saving time and money).

Joint tenants must obtain equal shares taking title to the property with the same deed and at the same time.

A deed, title, or other legally binding property ownership document spells out the terms of either a joint tenancy or tenancy in common.

If one tenant transfers interest to another person, the Joint Tenancy is broken, changing the ownership arrangement for all parties.

Joint Tenancy with Right of Survivorship

All owners take title at the same time with equal shares. Upon the death of one owner, the survivor takes over the whole property, avoiding any effect of a will, as well as probate. Clear title is given to the surviving joint tenant by usually recording an affidavit of survivorship and a certified copy of the death certificate.

In joint tenancy with right of survivorship, all co-owners must take the title at the same time. They must own equal shares. In the event of one owner's death, the surviving co-owner winds up owning the entire property. The deceased owner's will has no effect on joint tenancy property. The transfer of the property avoids the costs and delays of probate.

Living Trust

Probably one of the best ways to hold title to homes and other real property is in a revocable living trust, avoiding costs and delays of probate. A living trust can own multiple properties, as well as investments, and many things, with few disadvantages.

The creator of the trust (Trustor) is the person who places the property into the trust, and can deal with the property ordinarily, such as selling the property.

Upon the death of the creator/Trustor, the Alternative Trustor (named in the trust) takes over the assets to be distributed according to the terms of the trust. The terms of a Living Trust remain private, as well as being almost impossible to challenge by outsiders. Property in a Living Trust also receives a step-up basis, avoiding potentially substantial capital gains taxes to heirs. Laura, filed for divorce negotiating for the house she and her five daughters lived in. Laura took the title as Sole and Separate Property. Laura also bought another house which she also took as Sole and Separate property.

Upon Laura's diagnosis of a terminal illness, one daughter, Nicole, decided she deserved more "fairness" than her four sisters. She had her mother sign, only days before mom's death, the deeds of two properties to Nicole as A Married Woman, Sole and Separate Property. To make sure she didn't miss anything she downloaded a will off the internet and had her mother sign the will with her friends as witnesses. All, of course, without anyone else knowing.

An irony: by getting ownership to the property before her mother's death, there was no step-up in the cost basis. At the sale of the property a few months later, Nicole paid tax capital gains back to the date of her mother's purchase, a few hundred thousand dollars. If she had waited until the death of her mother, she would have received the property at the new current value by the will without any taxes.

The deeds and will were challenged in court. But after six months of bloodletting by fees, costs, and wasted time, the estate attorney simply advised to give up the challenge. Even if the challenge prevailed, there wouldn't be enough money to pay attorney fees. The only joy the jilted sister-heirs got: the capital gains and attorney fees burned through the proceeds of the house that was sold. And justice and fairness were served to all.

Well, except for the other house Nicole and her husband were living in. She had the property placed in her name as Sole and Separate Property at an extremely low value – most likely to avoid higher property taxes. This also raises her cost basis and will increase her capital gain tax substantially when she sells. This all would have been all avoided if she had not done the deed prior to her mother's death, and just given herself the deed from the deathbed will she concocted for herself.

Nicole is a stay at home mom. Any money from community property (accounts of her own and with her husband) she puts towards the house, will be considered commingling, and could raise a possible challenge to the Sole and Separate property by her husband – who probably got a real education watching his mischievous wife do the dirty deeds under-handing her four sisters.

> **Author's note to self**: Maybe Nicole's husband would like a copy of this book.

A living trust would have avoided these battles completely, and Laura's wishes would have been served.

A few frequent problems arise with living trusts. The first big mistake is not transferring properties and assets into the trust in the first place. Refinancing may require the property to be transferred out of the trust to get the loan. Then, the property must be transferred back into the trust. It is advisable to do an annual review of your living trust.

LLC – Limited Liability Corporation

A limited liability company is a separate, legal entity. This means that an LLC can hold title to real estate, obtain a tax identification number, open a bank account and do business, all under its own name. The primary advantage of an LLC is that its owners, known as members, have "limited liability," meaning that, under most circumstances, they are not personally liable for the debts and liabilities of the LLC.

A common mistake people make when considering an LLC is thinking an LLC protects them from outside nuisances such as lawsuits. LLC's safeguard from inside nuisances. Say you own a property in an LLC. If a tenant in the property sues, they will sue the LLC, exposing assets only within the LLC. If someone outside the LLC sues you, say like for insulting their dog, they can go after your ownership of the LLC.

In divorce, an LLC is looked at as an asset, being held by one of the above types of ownership. Beware of putting personal or community money into the LLC or paying LLC bills from community property or risk commingling.

A secret of the zillionaires:

"Control everything. Own nothing."

Nelson Rockefeller

Laws change frequently. Please seek the proper legal, financial advice pertaining to your own situation.

CHAPTER FIVE

What Is Your House Worth?

Who do you believe?

This is what this book is about. Money. Your money and how to keep it rather than watch slip through unknowing fingers, and how to put it towards your best interests. A home is often the most significant asset most people ever have.

There are several sources to establish values of real estate.

Online Evaluations

There are several broad-spectrum online property evaluations, such as Realtor.com, Zillow.com, Trulia.com, offering estimates of value. These take the information available through other online sources and process it through their "secret formula." If your house is pretty much like the rest of the houses around your house, as in condos, and there were several recent sales, these might come close.

Zillow came out with their internet property evaluation system in 2006. Electronic evaluation systems quickly took over the real estate lending price evaluations. Skipping the actual physical inspection of an appraiser saved lenders lots of money.

Inaccurate evaluations were a major cause of prices skyrocketing in the early 2000's. The battle cry was "real estate values in the United States never goes down. Lenders enticed borrowers with NINJA (no income, no job, no assets.) Prices continued to soar until borrowers couldn't make their loan payments collapsing property values, banks, and the whole economy.

Watch the movie <u>Inside Job</u> or read the book <u>The Big Short</u> (the movie was just a bit of character development missing the whole issue.)

In 2019, Zillow had a value for a three bedroom home in Gold Country California posted as $226,000. The property burnt to the ground in 2017.

Zillow posted the value of a San Francisco property in December 2018 at $2,355,000. Being on the market for 10 months, the property finally sold for $1,600,000, over 30% lower then Zillow 10 months before. Granted, the listing agent greatly overpriced the property, but so much for Zillow's secret formula.

Appraisers

Appraisers have substantially rigid guidelines, especially in their reports, to establish values. These guidelines have been established to maintain some sort of congruity in the banking evaluation systems. Appraisers usually have the

Michael Williamsen

benefit of actually seeing inside, measuring, and observing any amenities or adverse conditions of the subject property. Rarely have they seen inside the comparable property sales they use. Most often, they take the three most comparable sales and come up with some give-and-takes to compose their opinion of value. Very few real estate analysis methods account for local trends or insider information.

Insiders used to joke about the professional designation of being a Member of the Appraisal Institute, "**MAI**" as being: "Made As Instructed." Jokingly meaning that you can have whatever value you want on the appraisal as long as the check cleared.

The Appraisal Institute's own claim:

> MAI is a designation granted to appraisers by the Appraisal Institute. An appraisal prepared by an MAI is the most sought-after appraisal in the real estate industry. The MAI designation is respected by courts, lending institutions, government agencies, corporations, and other individuals desiring the highest quality of appraisal services. The Appraisal

68

Institute has been the world's leading organization of real estate appraisal professionals for more than 75 years, with over 25,000 members and 91 chapters throughout the world.

Make your own judgement on MAI. There were certainly many, many, appraisers, not of MAI designation, who have delivered less than truthful "appraisals."

Appraisers were certainly a link in the chain of destruction of the middle class in the last decade, as well as, real estate agents.

Comparative Market Analysis (CMA)

Most real estate agents use a CMA to estimate a sales price of the property once exposed to the open market by a willing buyer.

Agents will use information such as properties currently active, pending, and coming on the market. They may be able to get insider info on pending sales prices, sometimes substantially over asking price. A local insider agent will have a handle on this pulse, as well as local trends, and growth such as "path of progress."

Suggested List Price

Part of real estate agents' marketing strategies is to determine the listing price to encourage buyers to look at the house. Buyers are looking for the best value for their dollar. Ambitious sellers may over-price their houses hoping to catch that "perfect buyer."

Aggressive agents may underprice to get multiple offers to drive the price up, and get a quick commission.

> **Insider Tip:** If you go along with the underpricing method, make sure your house appeals to a large number of buyers. Overbidding does not work with only one buyer.

Fair Market Value

The price a willing buyer and a willing seller will agree upon to transfer the property is the ultimate test of value. Bottom line, buyers determine what they are willing to pay.

CHAPTER SIX

What Is Your House Really Worth?

Debts, Liabilities, Repairs, Maintenance, and Other Unsightly Issues

It is not uncommon to overrate the values of real estate. It **is** very common to undervalue the debt, liabilities, and repairs and conditions of the property.

Mortgages Most married couples are both on the mortgage:

"We are in this together, for better or worse."

is often the cry of allegiance at filling out the loan-application.

Your loan might have been paid down substantially, or it may have late payments piled up. In the 2007- 2010 era, spouses were sometimes ambushed, not knowing the debt on their community property.

> **Insider Tip**: It may be an advantage for one spouse to NOT be on the mortgage. On credit reports, both spouses are credited with the liability of the full amount of the mortgage; sort of a double-jeopardy. Also, sometimes one spouse has the higher income and credit, while the other spouse may not be so creditworthy. Putting the 2nd spouse on the mortgage could actually damage the ability to get the best loan.

One married couple had several million-dollar homes and a very successful business run by the husband. The wife also worked at a day job while raising the kids. The properties showed income and the business was flourishing.

Everything was glorious leading to their extravagant lifestyle. Upon their separation, she found the husband had taken out equity lines on all the properties, more than current diminished values, to keep the business going. An employee had been embezzling for years. The couple was bankrupt without the wife having a clue.

Found dead on his couch one warm afternoon, well, that will be in the next book on estates.

Equity Lines

Equity lines, or HELOCs (Home Equity Lines of Credit) were intended to be used to improve the house. Television ads boasted of buying cars, boats, vacations, and most everything on equity lines gaining the added bonus of having the tax deduction of the loan's interest. The

> **Insider Tip**: It can be an advantage for one spouse to buy the property as Sole and Separate Property, then put the 2nd spouse on title later.

following epic financial collapse of 2007 should not have been any surprise.

Construction Contracts

If you think construction is a mess, try keeping it going through a divorce. Some divorces are even caused by the construction.

Michael, a real estate agent who specialized in lots, got a great deal of calls from buyers wanting to build their "dream home." His response was published as the article, "Seven Sins of Dirt Deals."

The first sin: *"Sure, I can sell you a lot. But it won't be a dream. And I will re-sell your lot for you long before construction, then sell you two houses, a different one for each of you."*

Property Taxes

In California, we are blessed with Prop 13 which limits the amount property taxes can increase in a year. This may be a good thing. On the other hand, property taxes may not have been

> **Insider Tip:** You can check property taxes online. In Marin County, California https://apps.marincounty.org/TaxBillOnline

paid for several years. California will allow five years of back taxes to accumulate before taking action.

Insider Tip: Joy Hurtig, Vice President of Centergy Property Tax Reduction Strategies presents the following:

Paying property taxes IS an obligation... Overpaying is NOT."

Property Tax should be a consideration for divorce planning purposes. In California Proposition 13 places a ceiling on annual increases at a maximum of 2% per year, unless the property is sold, or title changes occur which can trigger reassessment.

A re-assessment of your original base year to the current fair market value can occur for a number of reasons beyond purchasing or selling your property. Reassessment can be triggered by a change of ownership or new construction.

There are change of ownership exceptions which include:

1) INTERSPOUSAL TRANSFERS This exemption includes legal entities owned by spouses.
2) TRANSFERS BETWEEN PARENTS AND CHILDREN on a personal residence and up to $1,000,000 of other real property such as commercial real estate (as long as filings with the county are timely and the value is assessed before death).
3) TRANSFERS BETWEEN GRANDPARENTS TO GRANDCHILDREN.

In order for these exemptions to hold, these interests must be held individually or in trusts, but NOT in business entities other than #1 above.

If you have substantial assets and are contemplating divorce, be aware there are many rules that govern transfers to or from legal entities, and, should always be reviewed by legal counsel.

These include Corporations, Limited Liability Companies, Limited Partnerships, transfers between Partners, Affiliated Corporations, and be aware that you should exercise extreme caution with Family Limited Partnerships. The rules surrounding California real property ownership changes are complex and a simple mistake can be very costly nullifying years of costly estate planning. If you are delinquent on your property taxes, California will allow you to defer payment (with penalties) of up to 5 years before the property will be sold for delinquent back taxes.

Joy Hurtig

Utilities, Services, and Suppliers

Utilities can vary widely throughout the year. Make sure you have all the numbers. Surprises can be chilling.

Personal Debts

"Till debt do we part."

Personal debt is most often considered community property, meaning both spouses are liable for the debt of each other, known or not. It may affect your net proceeds at settlement.

Property Condition

What about the house itself? Property condition will significantly affect value. This is often a substantial eye-opening reality check for a lot of people, especially when they love their home and can't imagine anything could possibly be wrong.

An owner had a charming, romantic, mountain cabin.

> **Insider Tip Property:**
> Disclosures and a walk-through form or rentals provided by a local real estate agent would be good starting lists to accumulate data on your house.
> Misrepresentation on disclosures is the number one cause of real estate lawsuits.

Allegedly, parents of a rock star once described it as "shimmering with history and old-world mystique." Being surrounded by its own Redwood Tree grove added magical powers. The trees were hanging over the house, their roots bared from soil erosion. One large Redwood branch had already torn a corner of the roof off. Covering up the damage provided the illusion of safety. Fence lines had been moved: almost assuring a property line dispute in the future. Smells of mold and mildew in the lower bedrooms were covered up by bleach and candles. Failed retaining walls holding up the rear yard had been covered by years of fallen tree branches and leaves. A loan modification was about to ripen.

Underneath the love and charm, houses are merely boxes sitting on a piece of dirt in a precise location. There are many ways these boxes lose their integrity. Water damage is the most common. The more you know about your house, the wiser decisions you will make.

Independent Construction Inspections

Termite/pest inspections, roof, pools, engineering, as well as many other investigations will reveal lots of hidden truths about a house.

You may reconsider taking over the property. Several clients took over ownership of the house, giving spouses other assets, only to find they couldn't afford the house.

Beth, divorced late in life, took over the family home. She called Rik, a loan broker, to help her refinance to get some more cash to live on. Upon his entry, he stepped around pots and pans catch rainwater coming through the roof. She had no job. She had no cash. Her credit was shot.

"You need to sell this house," Rik concluded.

"Not a chance," Beth replied. "They will take me out of this house feet-first in a box. What other advice do you have?"

Rik scanned the sea of pots and pans and said, "Home Depot has five-gallon buckets at five bucks."

Capital Gains

If your property went up in value, there might be Capital Gains Tax to pay. This can significantly reduce proceeds from an eventual sale. Capital gains are the amount of value your house went up since its purchase. Other factors come into play.

> **Insider tip:** You may get an exemption from all or part of your gains. Call your tax person. In general, if you lived in your house 2 of the past 5 years, a married couple may get, tax free, up to $500,000. Single people may get up to $250,000.

Cost Basis

This is what you originally paid for the house, plus capital improvements, plus or minus some varietal factors.

Capital Improvements

Capital improvements are major improvements such as additions, pools, and helicopter pads. Capital improvements are not painting, appliances, and things that wear out over the years, such as husbands and wives.

Mortgages

Mortgages have nothing to do with the cost basis.

Equity Lines

If you refinanced or took out an equity line, the mortgage is still irrelevant to capital gains. If you used those proceeds to add value to the house, then the costs of the improvements would be included as capital improvements.

A married couple bought a $400k house, and the value skyrocketed. They took out an equity line of $150k. Then they refinanced the house to pay off the equity line and give them a lower interest rate and some cash with a new loan of $600,000. To get some more cash, they took out a new equity line of $100k.

They divorced with the wife taking the house. The real estate market crashed. She lost her job. She couldn't afford $700k in mortgages and stopped making payments. Losing the house in foreclosure or selling were her only two options. Unfortunately, the value of the house was now $450k. She sold the house with a short sale process in which both the first mortgage and the equity line agreed to take a reduction in their proceeds from the sale.

Between 2007 and 2012, many people walked away from their houses and debt and let the house go through foreclosure. Some mortgages, especially refinance and equity lines, had personal liability clauses in tiny print on the notes that nobody read back in the day. This meant lenders could still go after the owner even if the owners lost the property by foreclosure. In some cases, even today in 2019, some lenders are threatening former homeowners with that tiny-print clause;

personal liability of the debt. States have a limit as to how long the lenders can go after the borrower, called a statute of limitations. In California, this limitation is currently four years from the last payment. If the borrower does not know this, they may be intimidated into writing a check. Threats often include a discount for an immediate payoff of the debt to avoid a lawsuit. Again, what we don't know can hurt us. Right?

In short sales, all mortgages were paid off at a discount and lenders waived their rights to go after owners. If the lender simply "wrote off the loss" or "mortgage forgiveness," as in foreclosure, they often sent a 1099 IRS form reporting the debt forgiveness as taxable income to the former owner.

Depreciation

> **Insider Tip:** Your tax preparer would know, or you can just check your IRS schedule E line 18. Make sure you check all years you owned the property.

If you have had ever rented out real estate, you may have taken tax write-offs described as depreciation. If you did, this write-off will be recaptured and added back into your gain and become taxable. This could be a substantial surprise.

Michael Williamsen

CHAPTER SEVEN

EVALUATION

This is not a test. This is your life.

You should have a reasonably good handle on the numbers. Add all the numbers together to find out the real value of your house. It is not uncommon for the spouse keeping the house to miscalculate and be forced to sell sooner than hoped.

It's fair to add value for, but don't expect anyone else to pay for:

1) Keeping the home in the family.
2) Keeping kids in the same home.

3) Knowing the house – good and bad.
4) Not dealing with the stress and cost moving.
5) Any other emotional attachments.

Ask yourself the following questions:

1) Is this a good investment?
2) Can you afford to keep and maintain this house considering all the costs and debts?
3) Is this a solid business decision or are you "following your heart?"
4) Might there be a better property that may fulfill your needs more effectively?
5) What are your options?

There are many online property search engines to look at alternatives such as:

Realtor.com

Zillow.com

Trulia.com

Realtor.com is the most closely associated with the real estate agents through the National

Association of Realtors (NAR) and will give the most current and accurate, publicly available information.

The other real estate search engines get most of their data from the real estate agents' Multiple Listing Service, with little or no accountability for being current or accurate. You may be looking at outdated or incorrect data. Their goal is to get your information to sell you as a lead back to the real estate agents who, ironically, provide the data to the search engines. The agent who gets your lead is the highest bidder for your criteria such as zip code, not the agent who would do the best job for you.

> **Insider Tip:** The best source is the actual Multiple Listing Service set up for you by a licensed agent to get sent newly posted listings. They may be able to give you an insider portal to do your own searches.

There is nothing better than to look at other properties in person. Look over neighborhoods. Are the houses well maintained? Look at the cars in the streets. Ask questions of people walking by.

Don't get caught in the staging trap. Staging is used to create perceived added value. It works.

CHAPTER EIGHT

KEEP THE HOUSE

To keep or not to keep. That is the question.

There are several possibilities of keeping the house as well as letting it go.

Keep the House Together with Neither Spouse in the House

Keep the house as a rental unit is one possibility. A property manager can simply do all the accounting, maintenance, and management and make a direct deposit into each spouse's bank accounts.

Keeping the property under common ownership has certain advantages as property taxes stay low due to California Prop 13. A change in ownership may cause a reassessment.

Income real estate offers unlimited write-off for taxpayers in the real estate profession. If you are not a real estate professional, you may deduct up to $25,000 per year against your personal income provided you comply with the rulings of an "active investor."

Keeping the same loan and interest rate may be an advantage. There will be no re-finance fees, and the loan term will have fewer years of repayment versus getting reset to 30 years.

Insider Tip: Another way to do this, after you are divorced, marry a real estate agent! But then would you seriously want to live with someone who goes through this stuff on a daily basis. Being in the real estate business itself is also a common source of divorces. My wife was also a real estate agent. Imagine the pillow talk.

Keep the House with One Spouse Remaining in the House

This has many issues, especially with kids or when one spouse owned the house prior to marriage.

Questions to answer yourself include bills, tax write-off, and maintenance.

One Spouse Buys Out the Other

> **Insider Tip**: Most people miss the re-set of the length of time when they refinance. They think just reducing their payments is a good thing. To get a fair comparison, the loans would need to be compared over the same amount of time. Loan brokers will hate this secret getting out.

Keep in mind, this is not just a question of keeping the house, one spouse will be buying out the other, in some form or another, or not.

Assume financing – The house can be transferred to one spouse by a quit-claim deed. The loan can stay in both names. Does this breach the loan agreement? That may be a question for your attorney or your own conscience. The problem, of course, is that the resident spouse may not make payments causing damage to the vacating spouse's credit. And, the mortgage debt stays on both spouses' credit report.

Seller financing – there is no law against one spouse taking their share as a note and deed of trust and receive monthly payments or accrue interest against the principle: sort of an equity partner but for a fixed amount.

> **Insider Tip:** Private auction between spouses may be a fun and exciting way of determining who keeps the house: Spouses bid back and forth with money or other property for their share of the house. Possibly fairer than just giving the house to one side. At least give the other side more money.

One couple filed for divorce. They had a multi-million-dollar business, a multi-million-dollar home, investment properties, a farm, stocks, bonds, IRAs, and on and on. This took a decade to sort out. Some divorces directly never reach a final settlement – they just give up, and each keeps what they have.

Maybe by now you just simply decide to walk away clean. Your next option: Sell.

Michael Williamsen

CHAPTER NINE

SELL

Is this an ending or a beginning?

The easiest way, especially for the real estate agent, is to sell the house vacant. One spouse staying in the house can be a conflict with the sale as they are getting a benefit, especially if the other spouse is paying the expenses. Making the house unavailable for showing, not keeping it in pristine condition, lack of cooperation can delay the sale and lessen the sale's price.

A motivated seller shows substantial effort to accommodate the deal, and prove cooperation between sellers, buyers, and agents.

One couple fought over who was to pay the mortgage, the loan went into foreclosure forcing the house to be sold as a desperation sale and at a discount.

> **Insider Tip**: A good real estate attorney should be able to whip you up a simple contract.

A simple agreement between spouses can help. Keep it clean, but complete and answer who pays expenses such as: mortgages, utilities, maintenance, upkeep and property taxes.

Pick an Agent

Divorces are already fraught with distrust and fear. For most agents, representing both parties in a divorce sale may seem like playing Russian Roulette with two single shot pistols pointed at their own head. Try not to put your agent in the place of being your friend or confidant—there are lots of bartenders who are great at that!

This is not the time to pick your best friend or family member as an agent. The potential for conflict of interest is enormous. You may struggle with the desire to give a friend a favor. This is the time for them to do you a favor: let you get the best representation possible for an already hostile situation. You can ask the agent to give your friend a referral fee. But you might consider if this may dampen the agent's enthusiasm to do their best job.

Agent Communication Ability

Insider Tip: Why Not Two Agents? It's odd how one agent will work hard on a $20k mobile home, but, refuse to split a listing on a Two Million Dollar home. Is it really that hard for us agents to get along with each other?

Communication between agent and both spouses is critical. Conflicts of interest are challenging in a typical deal for agents. Emails are a great way of communicating with both spouses as each sees the same message at the same time.

Marketing Plan

A good agent will establish a clear written plan, so that everyone knows what to expect in the marketing schedule and communications. Marketing real estate has several stages that can be somewhat predictable such as: timing the market, repairs, clean-up, staging, photographs, advertising, showing the house, when to expect offers and when to look at them, closing the escrow, moving out, and other stages.

Pricing

Don't make the mistake of merely going for the agent who gives you the highest price. It is the buyers who determine how much they will pay. Your listing agent can only suggest a list price to entice buyers to look at the house. Look at comparable listings and sales asking yourself, "if you were a buyer, which house would you take?"

One seller held on to the price of their over-priced house attaching added value to the peach tree as they had planted on the day that they moved into their love nest together.

Preparing the House

Clearing out the clutter, cleaning thoroughly, and fixing small things like door locks and latches, lightbulbs make first and lasting impressions. Start at the front yard, front door, and work your way through the house.

Insider Tip: You may never get through all the repairs you think may add value. Make up a list of all the improvements. Go over them with you agent prioritizing each task. Set a time limit. It may be more beneficial to not complete the list than to miss timing the market.

"You only have one chance for a first impression."

One investor spent so much time and money improving a property on things adding minimal value, he missed the market, paid more in interest and taxes and actually sold for a net loss.

Timing the market has a lot of variables such as demand, interest rates, weather, and even politics.

Disclosures

Disclosures are the biggest subject of real estate lawsuits. Many disclosures are mandatory by the state and cities. This is an excellent time to not add stress to your life by saving surprises for later. Sign all documents you can in advance shows the mutual effort to cooperate as well as reduced pressure and anxiety later for both sellers.

Have inspection reports available. If you have old reports, dig them up. If your house has problems, or you suspect problems, get new reports. There may be some simple things you can fix that will save some money, make your house more appealing, and avoid surprises. Conflicted owners don't need more shocks and stress.

> **Insider Tip**: House condition is a common cause for re-negotiations of the purchase price once the buyer gets their own reports. Agents call this "the mid-escrow grind."

Staging

Staging guru Barb Schwartz said, "You live in house differently than when the house is on the market for sale," and described staging in three categories: Clutter, Cleanliness, Color. Buyers expect a house to look near perfect. How a property appears is critical towards getting the best price. From the first impression to a pleasant memory,

> **Insider Tip**: You may be able to use your own furniture. Just keep to the "Clutter, Clean, and Clutter" theme.

staging makes the difference between being viewed as a house to a home. Statistics show that staged houses sell for more money and quicker than un-staged houses. Keep this in mind when you go to buy.

Showing the Property

An empty house is more accessible for other agents to show. Also, having someone living in the house can create problems with scheduling and keeping the property showing in its prime condition.

Kids are full of play and may leave toys distracting buyers.

Pets may even chase buyers and agents away. Some people are afraid animals and what they leave behind in their homes.

This may not be practical, and agents need to know they work for you, to satisfy your needs, not their desire for a quick and easy sale. Just be aware of the cost of someone staying in the house. The harder you make your house to view, fewer buyers will see it and the longer it will take. Time is definitely money in this situation.

Offers

Going for over-bidding is one strategy; underpricing the property to get buyers to bid against each other, playing off the old College Psych 101 phrase "greed and fear of loss." If your property is not one to attract multiple buyers, this strategy may not be desirable as you may get only one buyer who may have paid more, but why should they if they are the only bidder.

If you don't get offers in the first two weeks, don't expect multiple offers. You must decide if you are going to wait for the "perfect buyer" who may still be in diapers or reach into a new depth of buyers by lowering the price.

Negotiating

Buyers will believe they have a negotiating advantage if they think a seller is desperate. Some buyers will stay away from a divorce sale as they know it may be a challenge to close the sale when spouses disagree or may not cooperate in the deal to spite the other spouse.

Dave owned his home, got married, and got divorced. He decided to sell. A buyer made an offer which he accepted. The escrow company found out he had been recently divorced. Dave didn't have a copy of the divorce decree. The wife was not on title, but the escrow company required a quit claim deed from his spouse. Her signature was required. She refused and delighted in this opportunity to cause him more suffering. A copy of the divorce decree was found at the public records and escrow was satisfied. The buyer never knew all this drama was placing their purchase in danger. Had they known, would they have stayed in the deal?

Sale's Proceeds

What about the money?

Have a settlement agreement for proceeds. If you can't agree, place the proceeds in a trust account to be fought over later. Divorce attorneys have trust accounts. They also love knowing the money for their fees is already in their accounts. There are also third-party trusts to hold money.

OOPS?

What if you change your mind and decide not to sell? This is precisely the point as to why divorce deals are messy. Some agents will bite their lip, and let you out of the contract, in hopes and prayers you will repay the kindness when you next decide to sell.

Buyers may sue the owners for specific performance and/or damages.

When presented with this situation, with the property already in a contract to sell to a buyer, the selling couple decided to cancel the contract and stay in the house.

The listing broker's office manager told the sellers, *"sure, you may choose not to perform on the purchase contract you signed. As your agent, we have performed and expect to be paid. You can just make the check out to XYZ Realty."*

Michael Williamsen

CHAPTER TEN

WHERE ARE YOU GOING?

Your new home and how to get there.

Obviously, this will depend much on how well you survived the previous chapters.

Should you rent or buy?

What About the Stuff?

Don't fall in love with the house simply due to the interior, or the staging, basically other people's stuff.

Insider Tip: Alice Robertson is a Home Organizing Specialist and Owner of Tidy Home. Alice wrote the following article:

Declutter Your Home During Major Life Transitions by Alice Roberson

Major transitions provide you a chance to examine your life and rebuild it in positive ways. Simplifying life after a difficult time often means sorting through personal belongings. For example, you may be moving away from an ex-partner or buying a place across the country for a new job. Rather than keep everything, take the time to truly declutter. You'll not only have less to move, but your mental well-being will get a boost and you'll find yourself saying goodbye to some bad habits.

Clutter can become mentally consuming. It is hard to focus when you are surrounded by too much stuff and many people find themselves feeling irritable and exhausted when they live amid chaos.

U.S. News & World Report notes that people will often find that their anxiety and stress levels decrease when they declutter. Their sense of inner peace builds and they often feel more relaxed. In addition, you will likely feel liberated by taking control of your environment and ridding yourself of baggage, improving your state of mind.

Keeping only what is truly important to you will likely improve your decision-making skills, focus, and productivity. It is hard to stay positive and motivated to accomplish much if you are surrounded by reminders of negative things in your life, so cleaning house helps to clear your mind. Your creativity and confidence will soar and the sense of accomplishment you develop will spur you to make other positive changes. Decluttering is a great way to let go of your past and focus on your future. Get rid of items connected to your ex, former job, or stressful family members and focus on keeping only things you love or that motivate and inspire you. You will also want to ditch anything that makes you feel guilty or is connected to bad habits you are trying to break.

Evaluating what you keep and get rid of can also set the stage for healthier eating and better sleep. For example, if you need to stop eating junk food, declutter your kitchen and you'll likely feel more motivated to cook healthy foods in the well-organized space. Clear all of the piles of clothes off of your treadmill to gain a spark for exercise again, and your mind and body can better embrace quality rest when your bedroom is a peaceful, clean oasis.

If you find yourself struggling with a much-needed transition in life, like ending a toxic relationship or moving to a new home, embrace the chance to evaluate what is and is not working in your life and make significant changes. Let go of the fears, regrets, and failures that are tied to the clutter in your home and free yourself up for positivity and progress.

Alice Robertson

A successful accounting firm owner retired, got married, and traveled the world collecting wine with his new bride. They bought a multi million-dollar home with a San Francisco Bay view, and of course, a sizeable climate-controlled wine cellar. She brought her furniture to the new love nest.

Even wine couldn't keep them together, and they divorced. He bought her out of the house and all community property, but soon realized the house was no longer a home without his love. He put the property on the market for sale. The wife generously left her furniture in the house for staging purposes.

One day, while showing the house to potential buyers, the house was found completely empty. A call to the owner put him into a panic: "Check the wine cellar." It was completely empty. The wife had taken back her furniture. She had also figured he probably had drunk his half of the wine collection, so she helped herself to what was left. She was prosecuted for burglary.

Quite often, furniture and personal items have much more personal value than real value. Perhaps research the market value of furniture, tools, toys, and other personal items before you give up the house for them, or, fight over something of really no value.

www.Craigslist.com and www.EBay.com are great for finding values.

Often, the "Stuff" doesn't fit into the new home and is put into storage. Storage fees quickly surpass the values of items in storage.

Carmen got divorced and had to sell the house. She moved leaving many items for her kids. Her children fought over most everything, for sentimental reasons, except one old sketch in a simple frame. After the battle, the sketch was left on the curb for trash pickup. Her ex-husband drove by and picked up the sketch. He recognized as a sketch done of Carmen in Paris 17 years ago.

Choose wisely.

A loan broker will help you work out your budget based on your cash, income, and credit.

After William's divorce he had a real estate agent show him houses for several weeks. While writing an offer, the question was asked how he was going to pay for the house, William responded. "I will pay cash. I got a letter from Ed McMahon saying I have won a million dollars."

Small is the New Big. Many clients absolutely love the freedom from the demands of large homes.

Make your list of what you need, what you want, and what you are willing to comprise.

Moving

The best time to start moving is before you put your house on the market. Too much furniture will make the rooms appear small. Clutter will get in the way of buyers, give them a poor impression of the house. Stuffed closets will reflect as lack of storage. This all means less money for you.

Make some painful decisions which items go with you, which find new homes, and those going onto the afterworld of stuff. Letting go of items with emotional attachments are challenging and best done before the move. Storage companies are full of items owners couldn't find a use for or have the strength to let them go. Many times, the cost of storage far exceeds the replacement value of the items.

> **Insider Tip**: File boxes are a convenient size, sturdy, stackable, storable, and reusable.

A professional packer and mover once said, "Yes, your aunt's porcelain elephants are gorgeous and a great memory of her. But your memory only needs one elephant, not thirteen."

After the sale of their house, John expected to have to move all his belongings as well as his share of the community property and several trips to the dump. He walked into his home to find it thoroughly cleaned out by his spouse. He knew who took everything. Rather than fight over old stuff filled with unpleasant memories he decided to create a whole new environment for himself.

Maybe by now, you know the first step is to make your plan. Have a safe and prosperous new life.

"To sail the world, the first step is to pull your anchor."
Nautical Proverb

A Personal Message from the Author

Upon my personal change in marital status, I decided not to want to write another chapter to my old story. No one wanted to hear about my grief. Some were actually happy at my misery. Starting with a blank piece of paper, a whole new book unraveled, an entirely new story, a new romantic adventure. "Small" is the new "big" and simply quite peaceful and enjoyable.

My dad, a Lutheran Minister for 50 years, wrote a book called *Forgiveness*. The toughest chapter for me to accept was the chapter on "Forgive Yourself."

Hopefully, you have found peace in having a plan, understanding the processes, and have evaluated which battles to fight, which not to fight, and the cost and benefits of each step. Knowledge is truly power to minimize the stress and negativity of this stage of your life, re-evaluate your assets, and prepare for your future filled with joy and happiness -- perhaps a little wisdom.

Michael Williamsen

www.MarinBrokersGroup.com

MarinBrokersGroup.com was created to provide homeowners, buyers, sellers, investors, developers, and anyone interested in real estate with insider information in the form of video interviews. Top industry professionals are asked questions most would never ask. Their answers will inform and surprise you.

Marin Brokers Group can also be found on

Facebook   YouTube   Instagram

Insider Interview Videos are being added weekly on topics such as:

Estate Mistakes
- Kelley A. Way, Estate Attorney

Timing the Real Estate Market
- Carol Rodini, Real Estate Economist

Is This a Good Time to Buy Real Estate?
- Jeremy Forcier, Mortgage Broker

Boundary Disputes in Real Estate
- Steve Gainer, Real Estate Attorney

<u>Super Natural Home</u>
- Beth Greer, The Super-Natural Woman

<u>Reverse Mortgages</u>
- Mary Jo Lafaye

<u>Energy Healing for Real Estate</u>
- Ashima, Quantum Touch Practitioner

<u>Timing the Real Estate Market</u>
- Best of Investing Radio Talk Show

<u>Three Secrets to Successful Interior Design</u>
- Stacey Lapuk- National Award-Winning Interior Designer

<u>Overbidding In Real Estate</u>
- Michael Williamsen

More coming:

Selling for top dollar

Staging

Upgrades

Picking your agent

Affordable housing

Senior housing

Best time to sell real estate

Seven sins of dirt deals – vacant land

A few more people like you

Everyone in my transaction kept coming up with problems. Michael just came up with more solutions. His experience and honesty made me feel like everything was in control.
Kimberly, San Jose

Michael's creative ideas and solutions are amazing. A legend in the real estate business.
Michael McCall, President, Civil Consulting Group, Inc.

"Mike helped Lisa and me close 6 deals buying and selling. We keep coming back because his experience and creativity give us an advantage in the market. He is a trusted real estate expert's expert!"
Trini and Lisa – Northbay investors, winery owners

"Mike, You are always one step ahead of the market!"
Donna Russ, Financial Industry

My mother's passing this past year was very stressful. Dealing with her estate and home was even more stressful. Michael helped sort out the issues, ask the right people the right questions, and make informed decisions with the property. His calm presence helped deal with the stress. His experience, knowledge and wisdom guided me to make informed decisions feeling like it was in control.
Kim, San Rafael

"Mike, you have a long history of closing deals, and your number one strength is your ability to negotiate with difficult people. You personally do that by checking your ego at the door, putting your clients' best interests ahead of your own, and letting the other guy win small battles while you win the war. I have seen you in action many times. You are very good at what you do."
Dean Allen, Real Estate Broker and Harvard law student

Michael helped me with my recent purchase. He was very patient and often came up with creative ideas to smooth things out. Even after escrow closed, he continued to help me with problems at my new home. I will definitely use Michael again in my next purchase.

Kim Jones, Investor

I engaged Michael Williamsen's services to help me sell a lot in Kentfield, Ca. I live in San Diego. Michael did a very thorough job in all departments, especially concerning the finalization of the sale. He was particularly thorough in going over each and every document with me to make sure I knew what I was signing.

Lynne McCall, Retired

"Mike was a no-pressure agent who clearly had our best interests at heart. He was patient and had a real 'hands-on' approach with us to make sure we understood each issue and document and answered all of our questions."

Marci Rinkoff, Organizational Development & Coaching Programs Consultant

Mike helped my buy some properties in Napa in complicated situations. Mike kept the deal together with his persistence and positive attitude. His huge resource of experience helped too*!*

Richard Bicardo, Bicardo Builders, Napa, Sonoma, Marin

"Mike helped me make lots of money in many deals. He saved me from losing money in others. He really looks out for me!"

Robert - Investor/Developer, Marin/Sonoma

The sale of a home, under the best of circumstances, can be a chore. When the home is in Marin County, one owner is in Auburn and the other is in Los Gatos, it can be a real challenge. Mike's help, patience and attention to detail made it possible to complete the sale in a very timely manner. Thanks, Mike, for all your hard work.

Dave and Genie former absentee homeowners

As an owner of a local kitchen and bath supplier, I know lots of Realtors. When it came time to pick a Realtor to represent me in selling my old home, and helping me buy my new home, the obvious choice was Michael Williamsen. My dream property went into multiple offers. I wouldn't have gotten the house if not for Michael's great negotiation skills and patience.
Craig Holmstrand, owner of Kitchen and Bath store

"I felt like things were in control. His marketing plan and communication were wonderful."
Michael, San Rafael and Belvedere investor

"Mike sold my house for more than a recent appraisal then got me into my new house for less than the asking price!"
Alan R, San Marin County store owner

"We just loved Mike's written marketing plan. We sold for a record high in the complex! Michael's reparation and timing were the key."
Leonard & Narda, San Rafael

"The best investments I ever made were the ones I didn't make as one false move would have wiped me out. Mike keeps me out of the bad deals and into the deals that make me money. His market knowledge is essential to stay alive in this business."
Rob Fitzgerald, Developer, North Bay and Reno

"Why fool around with realtors that don't understand the complexities of Marin real estate. Mike's experience can make a big difference when buying and selling. He has smart clients who rely on his expertise and trust his advice. He has made a lot of money for a lot of people."
Anonymous Investor/developer

"We enjoyed and appreciated the professional assistance that Michael Williamsen provided us in both acquiring and selling our condominium in San Rafael. In each case he was thorough and hands-on regarding the details and providing advice. At the same time, we really enjoyed his personal warmth and friendliness. His extensive knowledge of the Marin County real estate market and the other "players" in this market was valuable to us, as well. We highly recommend Mike as a broker."
Charles and Sallie Wood, San Rafael

"Money has 3 steps: making it, keeping, and putting to work for you." *Mike Williamsen*

This space is reserved for your testimonial.

About the author

Michael Williamsen has been a real estate broker for over 35 years in Marin County, California, one of the wealthiest counties on the planet.

He has seen wealth elevate the ability to wage war over homes in numerous divorces.

This book was not a book Williamsen wanted to write but felt compelled to help clients survive their divorce and thrive in their new lives.

Even in the smallest real estate transaction, the emotional conflicts, stress, anxiety, all compound into confusion. Michael's intention in this book is to help you avoid destroying your financial future by empowering yourself with practical knowledge in order to make wise decisions, your own choices, for your personal best interests.

Michael Williamsen has also written:

We Played Baseball

Playing Catch with Destiny

Laura's War on Cancer

The Seven Sins of Dirt Deals

Real Estate Hangover 2019

The "F" Word in Real Estate

and numerous real estate articles

Interviewed several times on the radio talk show:

"Money Matters"

Michael received the National Award For

Marketing Excellence

by Realtor.com

Last Insider Tip: Michael can be reached at MikeWilliamsen@gmail.com

---

Michael Williamsen

Made in the USA
Columbia, SC
03 November 2019